NOAH
and the People of Faith

Contemporary Bible Series
NOAH and the People of Faith

Published by Scandinavia Publishing House 2009
Drejervej 15,3   DK-2400 Copenhagen NV, Denmark
Tel. (45) 3531 0330 Fax (45) 3536 0334
E-mail: info@scanpublishing.dk
Web: www.scanpublishing.dk

Text copyright © Contemporary English Version
Illustrations copyright © Gustavo Mazali
Design by Ben Alex
Printed in China
ISBN 978 87 7247 681 0

NOAH

and the People of Faith

Contemporary English Version

scandinavia

Contents

God Creates the World

In the beginning God created the heavens and the earth. The earth was barren, with no form of life; it was under a roaring ocean covered with darkness. But the Spirit of God was moving over the water.

God said, "I command light to shine!" And light started shining. God looked at the light and saw that it was good. He separated light from darkness. That was the first day.

God said, "I command a dome to separate the water above it from the water below it." And that's what happened. That was the second day.

God said, "I command the water under the sky to come together in one place, so there will be dry ground." And that's what happened. God looked at what he had done and saw that it was good.

God said, "I command the earth to produce all kinds of plants, including fruit trees and grain." And that's what happened. God looked at what he had done, and it was good. That was the third day.

God said, "I command lights to appear in the sky and to separate day from night and to show the time for seasons, special days, and years. I command them to shine on the earth." And that's what happened. God looked at what he had done, and it was good. That was the fourth day.

God Creates the Fish and the Birds

Genesis 1:20-23

God said, "I command the ocean to be full of living creatures, and I command birds to fly above the earth." So God made the giant sea monsters and all the living creatures that swim in the ocean. He also made every kind of bird. God looked at what he had done, and it was good. Then he gave the living creatures his blessing. He told the ocean creatures to live everywhere in the ocean and the birds to live everywhere on earth. Evening came and then morning—that was the fifth day.

God Creates the Animals

Genesis 1:24-25

God said, "I command the earth to give life to all kinds of tame animals. And that's what happened. Then he looked at what he had done, and it was good.

God Creates Man and Woman

Genesis 1:26-27; 2:7; 2:18-23; 1:28-2:3

God said, "Now we will make humans, and they will be like us. We will let them rule the fish, the birds, and all other living creatures." So God created humans to be like himself; he made man and woman. The LORD God took a handful of soil and made a man. God breathed life into the man, and the man started breathing.

The LORD God said, "It isn't good for the man to live alone. I need to make a suitable partner for him." So the LORD took some soil and made animals and birds. He brought them to the man to see what names he would give each of them. Then the man named the tame animals and the birds and the wild animals. That's how they got their names. None of these were the right kind of partner for the man. So the LORD God made him fall into a deep sleep, and he took out one of the man's ribs. Then after closing the man's side, the LORD made a woman out of the rib. The LORD God brought her to the man, and the man exclaimed,

"Here is someone like me! She is part of my body, my own flesh and bones. She came from me, a man. So I will call her woman!"

God gave them his blessing and said, "Have a lot of children! Fill the earth with people and bring it under your control. Rule over the fish in the ocean, the birds in the sky, and every animal on the earth. I have provided all kinds of fruit and grain for you to eat. And I have given the green plants as food for everything else that breathes. These will be food for animals, both wild and tame, and for birds."

God looked at what he had done. All of it was very good! That was the sixth day.

So the heavens and the earth and everything else were created. By the seventh day God had finished his work, and so he rested. God blessed the seventh day and made it special because on that day he rested from his work.

The Garden of Eden

Genesis 2:8-10; 2:15-17

The Lord made a garden in a place called Eden, which was in the east, and he put the man there. The Lord God placed all kinds of beautiful trees and fruit trees in the garden. Two other trees were in the middle of the garden. One of the trees gave life; the other gave the power to know the difference between right and wrong. From Eden a river flowed out to water the garden, then it divided into four rivers.

The Lord God put the man in the Garden of Eden to take care of it and to look after it. But the Lord told him, "You may eat fruit from any tree in the garden except the one that has the power to let you know the difference between right and wrong. If you eat any fruit from that tree, you will die before the day is over!"

Adam and Eve Disobey God

Genesis 3:1-7

The snake was sneakier than any of the other wild animals that the LORD God had made. One day it came to the woman and asked, "Did God tell you not to eat fruit from any tree in the garden?"

The woman answered, "God said we could eat fruit from any tree in the garden, except the one in the middle. He told us not to eat fruit from that tree or even to touch it. If we do, we will die."

"No, you won't!" the snake replied. "God understands what will happen on the day you eat fruit from that tree. You will see what you have done, and you will know the difference between right and wrong, just as God does."

The woman stared at the fruit. She wanted the wisdom that it would give her, and she ate some of the fruit. Her husband was there with her, so she gave some to him, and he ate it too. Right away they saw what they had done, and they realized they were naked. Then they sewed fig leaves together to make something to cover themselves.

Out of Eden

Genesis 3:8-13; 3:20-23

Late in the afternoon a breeze began to blow, and the man and woman heard the LORD God walking in the garden. They were frightened and hid behind some trees.

The LORD called out to the man and asked, "Where are you?"

The man answered, "I was naked, and when I heard you walking through the garden, I was frightened and hid!"

"How did you know you were naked?" God asked. "Did you eat any fruit from that tree in the middle of the garden?"

"It was the woman you put here with me," the man said. "She gave me some of the fruit, and I ate it."

The LORD God then asked the woman, "What have you done?"

"The snake tricked me," she answered. "And I ate some of that fruit."

The man Adam named his wife Eve because she would become the mother of all who live. The LORD said, "These people now know the difference between right and wrong, just as we do. But they must not be allowed to eat fruit from the tree that lets them live forever." So the LORD God sent them out of the Garden of Eden, where they would have to work the ground from which the man had been made.

Cain and Abel

Genesis 4:1-5

Adam and Eve had a son. Then Eve said, "I'll name him Cain because I got him with the help of the LORD." Later she had another son and named him Abel.

Abel became a sheep farmer, but Cain farmed the land.

One day, Cain gave part of his harvest to the LORD, and Abel also gave an offering to the LORD. He killed the first-born lamb from one of his sheep and gave the LORD the best parts of it. The LORD was pleased with Abel and his offering, but not with Cain and his offering. This made Cain so angry that he could not hide his feelings.

Cain Kills Abel

Genesis 4:6-16

The LORD said to Cain, "What's wrong with you? Why do you have such an angry look on your face? If you had done the right thing, you would be smiling. But you did the wrong thing, and now sin is waiting to attack you like a lion. Sin wants to destroy you, but don't let it!"

Cain said to his brother Abel, "Let's go for a walk." And when they were out in a field, Cain killed him.

Afterwards the LORD asked Cain, "Where is Abel?"

"How should I know?" he answered. "Am I supposed to look after my brother?"

Then the LORD said, "Why have you done this terrible thing? You killed your own brother, and his blood flowed onto the ground. Now his blood is calling out for me to punish you. And so, I'll put you under a curse. From now on, you'll be without a home, and you'll spend the rest of your life wandering from place to place."

So Cain had to go far from the LORD and live in the Land of Wandering, which is east of Eden.

Noah Builds a Boat

Genesis 6:5-22

More and more people were born, until finally they spread all over the earth.

The Lord saw how bad the people on earth were and that everything they thought and planned was evil. He was very sorry that he had made them, and he said, "I'll destroy every living creature on earth! I'll wipe out people, animals, birds, and reptiles. I'm sorry I ever made them." But the Lord was pleased with Noah, and this is the story about him. Noah was the only person who lived right and obeyed God. He had three sons:

Shem, Ham, and Japheth.

God knew that everyone was terribly cruel and violent. So he told Noah, "Cruelty and violence have spread everywhere. Now I'm going to destroy the whole earth and all its people. Get some good lumber and build a boat. Put rooms in it and cover it with tar inside and out. Make it four hundred fifty feet long, seventy-five feet wide, and forty-five feet high. Build a roof on the boat and leave a space of about eighteen inches between the roof and the sides. Make the boat three stories high and put a door on one side. I'm going to send a flood that will destroy

everything that breathes!
Nothing will be left alive. But
I solemnly promise that you,
your wife, your sons, and your
daughters-in-law will be kept
safe in the boat. Bring into the
boat with you a male and a
female of every kind of animal
and bird, as well as a male and a
female of every reptile. I don't
want them to be destroyed.
Store up enough food both for
yourself and for them."

   Noah did everything the LORD
told him to do.

Into the Boat

Genesis 7:1, 10, 13-16

The LORD told Noah, "Take your whole family with you into the boat, because you are the only one on this earth who pleases me."

Seven days later a flood began to cover the earth. On that day Noah and his wife went into the boat with their three sons, Shem, Ham, and Japheth, and their wives. They took along every kind of animal, tame and wild including the birds. Noah took a male and a female of every living creature with him, just as God had told him to do. And when they were all in the boat, God closed the door.

24

26

Safe Inside the Boat

Genesis 7:17-24; 8:1-19

For forty days the rain poured down without stopping. And the water became deeper and deeper, until the boat started floating high above the ground. Finally, the mighty flood was so deep that even the highest mountain peaks were almost twenty-five feet below the surface of the water. Not a bird, animal, reptile, or human was left alive anywhere on earth. The LORD destroyed everything that breathed. Nothing was left alive except Noah and the others in the boat.

A hundred fifty days later, the water started going down.

God did not forget about Noah and the animals with him in the boat. So God made a wind blow, and the water started going down. Forty days later Noah opened a window to send out a raven, but it kept flying around until the water had dried up.

Noah wanted to find out if the water had gone down, and he sent out a dove. Deep water was still everywhere, and the dove could not find a place to land. So it flew back to the boat. Noah held out his hand and helped it back in.

Seven days later Noah sent the dove out again. It returned in the evening, holding in its beak a green leaf from an olive tree. Noah knew that the water was finally going down. He waited seven more days before sending the dove out again, and this time it did not return.

Noah made an opening in the roof of the boat and saw that the ground was getting dry.

God said to Noah, "You, your wife, your sons, and your daughters-in-law may now leave the boat."

After Noah and his family had gone out of the boat, the living creatures left in groups of their own kind.

God's Promise to Noah

Genesis 9:1-16

God said to Noah and his sons, "I am giving you my blessing. Have a lot of children and grandchildren, so people will live everywhere on this earth. I am going to make a solemn promise to you and to everyone who will live after you. This includes the birds and the animals that came out of the boat. I promise every living creature that the earth and those living on it will never again be destroyed by a flood. The rainbow that I have put in the sky will be my sign to you and to every living creature on earth. It will remind you that I will keep this promise forever. When I send clouds over the earth, and a rainbow appears in the sky, I will remember my promise to you and to all other living creatures."

The Tower of Babel

Genesis 10:32-11:9

After the flood Shem, Ham, and Japheth's descendants became nations and spread all over the world.

At first everyone spoke the same language, but after some of them moved from the east and settled in Babylonia, they said, "Let's build a city with a tower that reaches to the sky! We'll use hard bricks and tar instead of stone and mortar. We'll become famous, and we won't be scattered all over the world."

But when the LORD came down to look at the city and the tower, he said, "These people are working together because they all speak the same language. This is just the beginning. Soon they will be able to do anything they want. Come on! Let's go down and confuse them by making them speak different languages—then they won't be able to understand each other."

So the people had to stop building the city, because the LORD confused their language and scattered them all over the earth. That's how the city of Babel got its name.

God Speaks to Abram
Genesis 12:1-9

The LORD said to Abram, "Leave your country, your family, and your relatives and go to the land that I will show you. I will bless you and make your descendants into a great nation. You will become famous and be a blessing to others. I will bless anyone who blesses you, but I will put a curse on anyone who puts a curse on you. Everyone on earth will be blessed because of you."

Abram was seventy-five years old when the LORD told him to leave the city of Haran. He obeyed and left with his wife

Sarai, his nephew Lot, and all the possessions and slaves they had gotten while in Haran.

When they came to the land of Canaan, Abram went as far as the sacred tree of Moreh in a place called Shechem. The LORD appeared to Abram and promised, "I will give this land to your family forever." Abram then built an altar there for the LORD.

Abram traveled to the hill country east of Bethel, where he built another altar and worshiped the LORD. Later, Abram started out toward the Southern Desert.

33

34

God's Promise to Abram

Genesis 15:1-7; 17:4-5

Later the LORD spoke to Abram in a vision, "Abram, don't be afraid! I will protect you and reward you greatly."

But Abram answered, "LORD All-Powerful, you have given me everything I could ask for, except children. And when I die, Eliezer of Damascus will get all I own."

The LORD replied, "No, he won't! You will have a son of your own, and everything you have will be his."

Then the LORD took Abram outside and said, "Look at the sky and see if you can count the stars. That is how many descendants you will have." Abram believed the LORD, and the LORD was pleased with him.

The LORD said to Abram, "I promise that you will be the father of many nations. That's why I now change your name from Abram to Abraham."

A Son for Abraham and Sarah

Genesis 18:1-15

One hot summer afternoon Abraham was sitting by the entrance to his tent near the sacred trees of Mamre when the Lord appeared to him. Abraham looked up and saw three men standing nearby. He quickly ran to meet them, bowed with his face to the ground, and said, "Please come to my home where I can serve you."

While they were eating, he stood near them under the trees, and they asked, "Where is your wife Sarah?"

"She is right there in the tent," Abraham answered.

One of the guests was the Lord, and he said, "I'll come back about this time next year, and when I do, Sarah will already have a son."

Sarah was behind Abraham, and she was listening at the entrance to the tent. Abraham and Sarah were very old, and Sarah was well past the age for having children. So she laughed and said to herself, "Now that I am worn out and my husband is old, will I really know such happiness?"

The Lord asked Abraham, "Why did Sarah laugh? Does she doubt that she can have a child in her old age? I am the Lord! There is nothing too difficult for me. I'll come back next year at the time I promised, and Sarah will already have a son."

Sarah was so frightened that she lied and said, "I didn't laugh."

36

The Sins of Sodom and Gomorrah

Genesis 18:16-32

When the three men got ready to leave, they looked down toward Sodom, and Abraham walked part of the way with them.

The LORD said, "Abraham, I have heard that the people of Sodom and Gomorrah are doing all kinds of evil things. Now I am going down to see for myself if those people really are that bad. If they aren't, I want to know about it."

Abraham asked, "LORD, when you destroy the evil people, are you also going to destroy those who are good? Wouldn't you spare the city if there are only fifty good people in it? You surely wouldn't let them be killed when you destroy the evil ones. You are the judge of all the earth, and you do what is right."

The LORD replied, "If I find fifty good people in Sodom, I will save the city to keep them from being killed."

Abraham said, "Please don't get angry, LORD, if I speak just once more. Suppose you find only ten good people there."

"For the sake of ten good people," the LORD told him, "I still won't destroy the city."

Lot Is Saved

Genesis 19:1-29

That evening the two angels arrived in Sodom, while Lot was sitting near the city gate.

The two angels said to Lot, "The LORD has heard many terrible things about the people of Sodom, and he has sent us here to destroy the city. Take your family and leave. Take every relative you have in the city."

Early the next morning the two angels tried to make Lot hurry and leave. At first, Lot just stood there. But the LORD wanted to save him. So the angels took Lot, his wife, and his two daughters by the hand and led them out of the city. The LORD sent burning sulfur down like rain on Sodom and Gomorrah. He destroyed those cities and everyone who lived in them, as well as their land and the trees and grass that grew there.

On the way, Lot's wife looked back and was turned into a block of salt.

When God destroyed the cities of the valley where Lot lived, he remembered his promise to Abraham and saved Lot from the terrible destruction.

Isaac Is Born

Genesis 21:1-7

The LORD was good to Sarah and kept his promise. Although Abraham was very old, Sarah had a son exactly at the time God had said. Abraham named his son Isaac. Abraham was a hundred years old when Isaac was born, and Sarah said, "God has made me laugh. Now everyone will laugh with me. Who would have dared to tell Abraham that someday I would have a child? But in his old age, I have given him a son."

Abraham and Isaac

Genesis 22:1-5

Some years later God decided to test Abraham, so he spoke to him.

Abraham answered, "Here I am, LORD."

The LORD said, "Go get Isaac, your only son, the one you dearly love! Take him to the land of Moriah, and I will show you a mountain where you must sacrifice him to me on the fires of an altar."

So Abraham got up early the next morning and chopped wood for the fire. He put a saddle on his donkey and left with Isaac and two servants for the place where God had told him to go.

Three days later Abraham looked off in the distance and saw the place. He told his servants, "Stay here with the donkey, while my son and I go over there to worship. We will come back."

God Spares Isaac

Genesis 22:6-13; 15-18

Abraham put the wood on Isaac's shoulder, but he carried the hot coals and the knife.

As the two of them walked along, Isaac said, "Father, we have the coals and the wood, but where is the lamb for the sacrifice?"

"My son," Abraham answered, "God will provide the lamb."

The two of them walked on, and when they reached the place that God had told him about, Abraham built an altar and placed the wood on it. Next, he tied up his son and put him on the wood. He then took the knife and got ready to kill his son. But the LORD's angel shouted from heaven, "Abraham! Abraham!"

"Here I am!" he answered.

"Don't hurt the boy or harm him in any way!" the angel said. "Now I know that you truly obey God, because you were willing to offer him your only son."

Abraham looked up and saw a ram caught by its horns in the bushes. So he took the ram and sacrificed it in place of his son.

The LORD's angel called out from heaven a second time, "You were willing to offer the LORD your only son, and so he makes you this solemn promise, 'I will bless you and give you such a large family, that someday your descendants will be more numerous than the stars in the sky or the grains of sand along the beach. They will defeat their enemies and take over the cities where their enemies live. You have obeyed me, and so you and your descendants will be a blessing to all nations on earth.'"

A Wife for Isaac
Genesis 24:1-27

Abraham was now a very old man. The LORD had made him rich, and he was successful in everything he did. One day, Abraham called in his most trusted servant and said to him, "Go back to the land where I was born and find a wife for Isaac from among my relatives."

Soon after that, the servant loaded ten of Abraham's camels with valuable gifts. Then he set out for the city in northern Syria, where Abraham's brother Nahor lived.

When he got there, he let the camels rest near the well outside the city. It was late afternoon, the time when the women came out for water. The servant prayed, "You, LORD, are the God my master Abraham worships. Please keep your promise to him and let me find a wife for Isaac today. The young women of the city will soon come to this well for water, and I'll ask one of them for a drink. If she gives me a drink and then offers to get some water for my camels, I'll know she is the one you have chosen."

While he was still praying, Rebekah walked past Abraham's servant, and filled her water jar. When she started back, Abraham's servant ran to her and said, "Please let me have a drink of water."

"I'll be glad to," she answered. Then she quickly took the jar from her shoulder and held it while he drank. After he had finished, she said, "Now I'll give

your camels all the water they want." Abraham's servant did not say a word, but he watched everything Rebekah did, because he wanted to know for certain if this was the woman the LORD had chosen.

The servant had brought along an expensive gold ring and two large gold bracelets. When Rebekah had finished bringing the water, he gave her the ring for her nose and the bracelets for her arms. Then he said, "Please tell me who your father is. Does he have room in his house for me and my men to spend the night?"

She answered, "My father is Bethuel the son of Milcah and Nahor. We have a place where you and your men can stay, and we also have enough straw and feed for your camels."

Then the servant bowed his head and prayed, "I thank you, LORD God of my master Abraham! You have led me to his relatives and kept your promise to him."

49

Isaac and Rebekah
Genesis 24:28-67

Rebekah ran straight home and told her family everything. Her brother Laban heard her tell what the servant had said and ran out to Abraham's servant. Then Laban said, "The LORD has brought you safely here. Come home with me. I have a room ready for you in our house, and there's also a place for your camels."

Abraham's servant went home with Laban, where Laban's servants unloaded his camels. After that, they brought in food. But the servant said, "Before I eat, I must tell you why I have come."

"Go ahead and tell us," Laban answered. The servant explained. Laban and Bethuel answered, "The LORD has done this. Take Rebekah with you; she can marry your master's son, just as the LORD has said."

Rebekah and the young women who were to travel with her prepared to leave. Then they got on camels and left with Abraham's servant and his men.

One evening Isaac was walking out in the fields, when suddenly he saw a group of people approaching on camels. So he started toward them. Rebekah saw him coming; she got down from her camel, and asked, "Who is that man?"

"He is my master Isaac," the servant answered. Then Rebekah covered her face with her veil.

The servant told Isaac everything that had happened. Isaac took Rebekah into the tent where his mother had lived before she died, and Rebekah became his wife. He loved her and was comforted over the loss of his mother.

Jacob and Esau Are Born

Genesis 25:19-26

Isaac was the son of Abraham, and he was forty years old when he married Rebekah. Almost twenty years later, Rebekah still had no children. So Isaac asked the LORD to let her have a child, and the LORD answered his prayer.

Before Rebekah gave birth, she knew she was going to have twins because she could feel them inside her, fighting each other. She thought, "Why is this happening to me?" Finally, she asked the LORD why her twins were fighting, and he told her, "Your two sons will become two separate nations. The younger of the two will be stronger, and the older son will be his servant."

When Rebekah gave birth, the first baby was covered with red hair, so he was named Esau. The second baby grabbed on to his brother's heel, so they named him Jacob.

53

Jacob Cheats Esau

Genesis 25:27-34

As Jacob and Esau grew older, Esau liked the outdoors and became a good hunter, while Jacob settled down and became a shepherd. Esau would take the meat of wild animals to his father Isaac, and so Isaac loved him more, but Jacob was his mother's favorite son.

One day, Jacob was cooking some stew, when Esau came home hungry and said, "I'm starving to death! Give me some of that red stew right now!"

Jacob replied, "Sell me your rights as the first-born son."

"I'm about to die," Esau answered. "What good will those rights do me?"

But Jacob said, "Promise me your birthrights, here and now!" And that's what Esau did. Jacob then gave Esau some bread and some of the bean stew, and when Esau had finished eating and drinking, he just got up and left, showing how little he thought of his rights as the first-born.

Isaac Blesses Jacob

Genesis 27:1-40

After Isaac had become old and almost blind, he called in his first-born son Esau.

Isaac said, "I am old and might die at any time. So take your bow and arrows, then go out in the fields, and kill a wild animal. Cook some of that tasty food that I love so much and bring it to me. I want to eat it once more and give you my blessing before I die."

Rebekah had been listening, and as soon as Esau left to go hunting, she said to Jacob, "Go and kill two of your best young goats and bring them to me. I'll cook the tasty food that your father loves so much. Then you can take it to him, so he can eat it and give you his blessing before he dies."

"My brother Esau is a hairy man," Jacob reminded her. "And I am not. If my father touches me and realizes I am trying to trick him, he will put a curse on me instead of giving me a blessing."

Rebekah insisted, so Jacob brought the meat to his mother, and she cooked the tasty food that his father liked. Then she took Esau's best clothes and put them on Jacob. She also covered the smooth part of his hands and neck with goatskins and gave him some bread and the tasty food she had cooked.

Jacob went to his father and said, "Father, here I am."

"Which one of my sons are you?" his father asked.

Jacob replied, "I am Esau, your first-born, and I have done what you told me."

Isaac asked, "My son, how did you find an animal so quickly?"

"The LORD your God was kind to me," Jacob answered.

"My son," Isaac said, "come closer, where I can touch you and find out if you really are Esau."

Jacob went closer. His father touched him and said, "You sound like Jacob, but your hands feel hairy like Esau's." And so Isaac blessed Jacob, thinking he was Esau.

Right after Isaac had given Jacob his blessing and Jacob had gone, Esau came back from hunting. He cooked the tasty food and brought it to his father.

"Who are you?" Isaac asked. "I am Esau, your first-born son."

Isaac started trembling and said, "Then who brought me some wild meat right before you came in? I ate it and gave him a blessing that cannot be taken back."

Esau cried loudly and begged, "Father, give me a blessing too!"

Isaac answered, "Your brother tricked me and stole your blessing."

"Father," Esau asked, "don't you have more than one blessing? You can surely give me a blessing too!" Then Esau started crying again.

Rebekah Sends Jacob Away

Genesis 27:41-45

Esau hated his brother Jacob because he had stolen the blessing that was supposed to be his. So he said to himself, "Just as soon as my father dies, I'll kill Jacob."

When Rebekah found out what Esau planned to do, she sent for Jacob and told him, "Son, your brother Esau is just waiting for the time when he can kill you. Now listen carefully and do what I say. Go to the home of my brother Laban in Haran and stay with him for a while. When Esau stops being angry and forgets what you have done to him, I'll send for you to come home. Why should I lose both of my sons on the same day?"

58

Jacob's Dream

Genesis 28: 10-19

Jacob left the town of Beersheba and started out for Haran. At sunset he stopped for the night and went to sleep, resting his head on a large rock. In a dream he saw a ladder that reached from earth to heaven, and God's angels were going up and down on it. The LORD was standing beside the ladder and said, "I am the LORD God who was worshiped by Abraham and Isaac. I will give to you and your family the land on which you are now sleeping. Your descendants will spread over the earth in all directions and will become as numerous as the specks of dust. Your family will be a blessing to all people. Wherever you go, I will watch over you, then later I will bring you back to this land. I won't leave you—I will do all I have promised."

Jacob woke up suddenly and thought, "The LORD is in this place, and I didn't even know it." Then Jacob became frightened and said, "This is a fearsome place! It must be the house of God and the ladder to heaven."

When Jacob got up early the next morning, he took the rock that he had used for a pillow and stood it up for a place of worship. Then he poured olive oil on the rock to dedicate it to God, and he named the place Bethel.

The Contemporary Bible Series